Steamers to Ayrshire

Andrew Clark

The car ferry *Glen Sannox* arrives at Ardrossan's Winton Pier on 6 April 1974.

Text © Andrew Clark, 2018.
First published in the United Kingdom, 2018,
by Stenlake Publishing Ltd.
Telephone: 01290 551122
www.stenlake.co.uk

ISBN 9781840338171

The publishers regret that they cannot supply copies of any pictures featured in this book.

THE GLASGOW STEAM BOAT

SAILS from this on SATURDAY NEXT, at seven o'-
clock morning, for GREENOCK, GOUROCK,
LARGS, and ARDROSSAN, and returns to Glasgow on
Monday.
    Glasgow, Sept. 6, 1815.

. WANTED. FOR A COTTON MILL.

An early advertisement for the first steamer to operate on the Largs trade. Built in 1813, a year after the pioneering *Comet*, *Glasgow* was the fourth steamboat on the Clyde. She continued in service until the early 1830s.

Acknowledgements

Images from the Geoffrey Grimshaw Collection are reproduced by courtesy of the McLean Museum, Inverclyde Council, and from the Roy Hamilton, Dr Joe McKendrick and CRSC Digital Collections by courtesy of the Clyde River Steamer Club. Other illustrations were kindly provided by A.E. Bennett, Walter Bowie, Ian Duncan, Graham Lappin, Lawrence Macduff, William MacDonald, Fraser MacHaffie, Ian Milne, Eric Schofield, the J.T.A. Brown Collection and the Sinclair Collection. Additional help came from Iain MacLeod, John Newth, Craig Osborne and Lawrie Sinclair.

Adder and *Duchess of Hamilton* depart Ardrossan *circa* 1894 – one sailing to Belfast, the other to Brodick. Each played a significant role in developing services from Ayrshire to Northern Ireland and Arran respectively.

Introduction

The heyday of Clyde pleasure cruising lasted from the 1890s to the 1950s, two world wars excepted. In summer you could sail from Ayr, Troon and Ardrossan to all corners of the firth – Rothesay one day, Arrochar the next, a Kyles pier the day after. For much of that period Stranraer and Loch Fyne were also within reach. By careful timetable planning, you could leave Ayr at 10am and return before dark on the same ship, having 'bagged' up to 10 other steamers in the course of the day. Morning and evening, the piers at Fairlie and Largs were abuzz with comings and goings. Even Girvan boasted an excursion programme which, on a handful of dates throughout the summer, enabled day trippers to sample the best of the Clyde's scenery.

While Ayrshire's coastal communities never stood at the epicentre of Clyde cruising, they were spoilt in the half-century before the motor car became commonplace: they themselves were destinations as well as departure points, and when the summer sun went down they served a different purpose to most of their up-firth counterparts. Unlike Dunoon or Rothesay, the towns of Ayr, Troon and Ardrossan were working ports, their year-round trade continuing in defiance of the southerly and sou'westerly storms battering them in winter, against which elaborate breakwaters had long provided protection.

Their shipping interests extended well beyond the coasting trade and the herring industry. Together with Irvine, and to a lesser extent Girvan and Fairlie, these towns had shipbuilding and repair businesses, renowned far afield but also patronised by local shipowners. The Ardrossan Dockyard, for example, built MacBrayne's *Loch Carron* and the Caledonian Steam Packet Company's *Maid of Cumbrae*. The Ailsa yard at Troon gave birth to the 1957 *Glen Sannox* and the 2000 *Lochnevis*, and was used for annual overhauls.

The changing character of these ports over the past 50 years reflects the evolving patterns of our lives. The motor car and the foreign holiday have taken over to a degree our mid 20th century forebears could never have imagined. Where seasonal excursion steamers once proliferated, year-round point-to-point ferries now hold sway. Yacht marinas have replaced wooden piers as the gateway to pleasure pursuits on the water. The Clyde is no longer the cradle of shipbuilding or a hive of fishing.

And yet the thrill of setting off from the mainland on the sea journey to Arran has not changed over the course of time, any more than the attraction of heading out from the Ayrshire coast on a paddle steamer to get a close-up of Ailsa Craig's granite facades: *Waverley* continues to offer this trip on a handful of occasions each summer, in remarkable defiance of her age.

My own experience of Ayrshire ports adds up to a lifetime of memories. I can still hear the hammers ringing out over Troon Harbour in 1957 as the shipbreakers set to work on the beautiful cross-channel turbine steamer *Lairds Isle*. In my mind's eye I can picture a contented crowd pouring off *Duchess of Hamilton* and boarding a special train at Fairlie Pier after a charter cruise in the early 1960s, courtesy of the Saxone Shoe Company in Kilmarnock where my father worked. And I will never forget the Isle of Man steamer *Lady of Mann* moving majestically stern-first out of Ardrossan Harbour in August 1971, her red and black funnel gleaming in the sun against a backdrop of the Arran hills, before she sped off towards the southern horizon on her final public sailing.

Although Ayrshire's ports today are much quieter than in their late 19th and early 20th century heyday, their sturdy harbour walls stand as a monument to a bustling, energetic past and an open invitation for us to listen at leisure to the call of the sea that gave them life.

Andrew Clark
Glasgow, June 2018

THE BRISBANE PICTURE OF LARGS IN 1845.

After steamboats from Glasgow reached the Ayrshire coast in 1815, links with the outside world took a leap forward. This was three years after the pioneering voyage of Henry Bell's *Comet*, the first mechanically powered vessel to operate commercially in open waters. *Comet* ran only from Glasgow to Greenock and Helensburgh, but soon steamboats were sailing the length and breadth of the Clyde estuary. Largs was one of the first coastal towns to be connected to Glasgow by steamer – a quicker and more comfortable means of transport than mail coach or covered wagon. In 1832 a pier was built, allowing steamers to call at all states of the tide, and although Largs was soon eclipsed by Rothesay as the Clyde's most popular resort, it remained an important calling point for vessels heading for Millport, Ardrossan, Arran and beyond. Trade was dominated by Captain Duncan McKellar's boats, initially boasting martial names like *Hero* and *Warrior*. The picture above features two steamers built by a rival company in the early 1840s, *Lady Kelburne* and *Lady Brisbane*, which were the first to make possible a return journey to Glasgow in a single day. Their debut triggered a period of cut-throat competition, ending with a merger of the two fleets. The ageing Captain McKellar finally sold out in the late 1860s because of rising competition from a new fleet of steamers based at Wemyss Bay.

By the 1880s Largs was well established as a Clyde resort, with a variety of steamers visiting its L-shaped stone pier. The most frequent callers were members of the Gillies and Campbell fleet, such as *Argyle* and *Lancelot* – seen here on a particularly busy day *circa* 1885 against the backdrop of a yacht regatta. James Gillies and his son-in-law Alexander Campbell were steamboat captains who had picked up the pieces of the Greenock and Wemyss Bay Railway Company's failed steamer-operating offshoot in the late 1860s. Thanks to their local knowledge and entrepreneurial flair, the two captains built a successful no-frills business, but when the big railway companies muscled in on the Clyde steamer trade in 1889-90, Gillies and Campbell were unable to compete. *Argyle*, distinguished by her attractive canoe-like bow (outer berth), was a flush-decked steamer, with covered accommodation confined to small cabins below the waterline. Lancelot (closest to pier) had a raised quarterdeck – a fashion of the late 1860s and 1870s, whereby the deck aft of the engine room was raised to create a proper cabin with portholes or windows. Both steamers were sold off the Clyde in 1890.

Benmore leaves Ayr astern *circa* 1890. Ayr was a busy port long before the arrival of steam, and its trading links with Kintyre, Galloway and Ireland continued to flourish after the arrival in 1840 of the railway, which reduced the importance of the town's sea connection with Glasgow. Excursions out of Ayr began as early as 1827, when the steamer *Leven* was advertised to cruise round Ailsa Craig. Similar trips continued for much of the 19th century, and it was not until the advent of *Bonnie Doon* in 1876 that regular cruises to and from Ayr took place throughout the summer season (see facing page). *Benmore*, built at Rutherglen in 1875 for the Holy Loch trade, became a regular visitor to Ayrshire ports in the late 1880s under the ownership of Captain William Buchanan. On Saturday 27 July 1889, for example, she sailed from Irvine and Ardrossan to Arrochar via the Kyles of Bute. Two days later she left the same ports for a cruise round Arran to Campbeltown. After the arrival of more sophisticated railway steamers in the 1890s, a vessel with limited deck cover could no longer compete in the open seas of the lower Firth, and *Benmore* was assigned to the 'doon the watter' trade from Glasgow. She remained in service until 1920.

No account of cruising out of Ayr could fail to mention a 19th century paddler known, unfairly, as 'Bonnie Breakdoun'. This was the 1876 *Bonnie Doon*, an appropriate name for a paddler built to serve the port near where the River Doon enters the sea. As well as operating her owner's Glasgow-Ayr summer service, she undertook early season pleasure trips from Ayr to Arrochar, Lochgoilhead and other distant piers – to which her speed, her solid constitution and aft deck saloon made her well suited. There is no evidence that she suffered more frequent mechanical failure than any other steamer of the period. The reason for her less than glorious reputation may be the fact that, after being sold in 1880 to North Wales, she went through a quick succession of owners, none of whom was able to make profitable use of her. Her only period of stability came at the end of her career, when the Clyde-born brothers Peter and Alec Campbell used her on their Bristol Channel services for 14 years – until she was broken up 1913. It is in their colours that she is pictured *circa* 1900.

Caledonia arrives at Largs *circa* 1890. This was the dawn of the 'golden years' of the Clyde steamers, a period characterised by ruthless ambition and ruinous competition between railway companies, lasting until the outbreak of war in 1914. During this time most of the small, privately owned fleets that had predominated in the 1870s and 1880s were elbowed out by mighty railway companies, which spared no expense to capture their share of the rapidly expanding Clyde steamer trade. The Caledonian Steam Packet Company (CSP), an offshoot of the Caledonian Railway, muscled in on the Ayrshire coast, and *Caledonia* of 1889 was its first new-build, quickly establishing herself on the Millport run from the railhead at Wemyss Bay. A pretty little boat that later became associated with the Holy Loch run, *Caledonia* had a long and remarkably uneventful life, lasting until the end of the 1933 season.

The Caledonian Railway's main competitor was the Glasgow and South Western Railway (G&SWR or 'the Sou'West'). In 1882 the Sou'West established a railhead at Fairlie, reached by a circuitous route via Kilwinning and Ardrossan, with an extension to Largs in 1885. The pier at Fairlie was a solidly built wooden structure, 300 feet long with a T-shaped head measuring 200 feet by 30 feet. Initially the Sou'West relied on a private operator to provide onward sea connections to Millport and Kilchattan Bay. Outsmarted by the Caledonian advance in 1889-90, the G&SWR quickly secured the legal right to operate its own fleet and snapped up a group of second-hand steamers, which it proceeded to brighten up and modernise. One of them was *Marquis of Bute*, built in 1868 and based at Fairlie from 1892. She is pictured there in her attractive new G&SWR livery – lavender grey hull, white upper works and red funnel with black top. *Marquis of Bute* was a useful steamer with a small deck saloon and a handy turn of speed. After being succeeded by *Vulcan* (better known as *Kylemore*) in 1904, she operated for three years in Ireland before being broken up in 1908.

Duchess of Hamilton passes Ailsa Craig *circa* 1895. Competition between the Clyde's railway-owned fleets was at its most cut-throat on the Ardrossan-Arran run. Before 1890 this had been in the hands of private operators, working in harness with G&SWR rail connections at Ardrossan's Winton Pier. In 1890 the CSP brought out the magnificent *Duchess of Hamilton*, operating from a new railhead at Montgomerie Pier and quickly capturing most of the trade. Although her profile was too stiff to be graceful, *Duchess of Hamilton* was beautifully fitted out and looked handsome in the CSP's livery of all-yellow funnel, blue-black hull with two gold lines just below rail level, and white paddle-boxes with blue name boards and gold ornamentation. She also represented an advance in paddle steamer design by having her promenade deck carried all the way to the bow, though the foremost part was not plated in, to allow the handling of ropes on the main deck. In the middle of the day *Duchess of Hamilton* undertook weekday excursions from Ardrossan, cruising round Ailsa Craig on Wednesdays. From 1906, when the CSP's first turbine steamer, *Duchess of Argyll*, replaced her at Ardrossan, the 'Hamilton' operated out of Gourock. She was requisitioned for war service in 1915 and mined off Harwich on 29 November that year.

Neptune at Ayr in 1896, the first of her two summers as Ayr excursion steamer. She was the first new boat built by the Sou'West in its attempt to claw back business from the CSP. Built to a proven design and launched on 10 March 1892, *Neptune* took up the Ardrossan-Arran run barely a month later, immediately engaging in a series of ding-dong battles with *Duchess of Hamilton*. By achieving a crossing time of 39 minutes (and on one occasion, 15 April 1892, 38 minutes), she made possible a 95-minute service from Glasgow to Brodick. After being succeeded in June by the first *Glen Sannox*, *Neptune* was based at Greenock for the next four summers, returning to the Ayrshire coast in 1896 and 1897 as the Ayr excursion steamer, in which role she ranged as far afield as Arrochar and Stranraer. A minesweeper in the First World War, she was blown up off the French-Belgian coast on 20 April 1917.

Adder and *Glen Sannox* at Ardrossan *circa* 1895. Both steamers set new standards for speed and comfort. Built by Fairfields in 1890, *Adder* was designed for G. &. J. Burns' daytime return service to Belfast, then in its infancy. Initially she sailed from Greenock, painted in the customary Burns colours of all-black funnels, hull and paddle-boxes, but after the extension of Ardrossan Harbour in 1892 she moved there, with a new colour scheme of yellow funnels with black top and white paddle-boxes and sponsons. Leaving Ardrossan at 10am and returning at 8.30pm, she cut the sailing time to Belfast to four hours. Like *Adder*, *Glen Sannox* was credited with a top speed of 20 knots. Launched on 26 March 1892 at J. & G. Thomson's Clydebank yard (later John Brown's, builder of the Cunard 'Queens'), the 'Sannox' was the G&SWR's emphatic response to the CSP challenge on the Arran run. On her entry into service on 6 June she made the crossing to Brodick in 33½ minutes, a feat achieved at the cost of extravagant fuel consumption. The journey time to Glasgow off the 8.05am sailing from Brodick was reduced to just 80 minutes.

Glen Sannox was the most opulent steamer ever built for Clyde service. She had a striking appearance, with two tall, slim funnels placed fore and aft of majestically tapered paddle-boxes, and plating carried up to promenade deck level at the bow – a first for the Clyde. Her visits to Ayr were rare, so her arrival here was probably for a special excursion – such as the Ayrshire Wine and Spirit Trade Association's charter on Wednesday 26 June 1895, which took 700 passengers from Ayr to Strachur in Loch Fyne, via Ardrossan, Keppel, Largs and the Kyles of Bute. "It is not our intention to dwell at length on the manifold beauties of sea and land and sky which constantly meet the eye on this route," reported the *Ardrossan and Saltcoats Herald* two days later, "but in order that the charm of the scenery may be realised to the full, it is a necessity that it be viewed from the deck of a passing steamer. The purveying was excellent in quality and service, this important feature being admirably looked after by Mr Colin McLellan, superintendent steward, and Mr E. Somerville, the chief steward. The fine music discoursed by the string band of the steamer was greatly appreciated, some of the younger folks footing it gracefully and merrily to the lively strains."

Portencross was the shortest-lived of all Clyde piers in regular use. It opened in 1912 and closed after war broke out in 1914. Unlike many wooden piers that had a longer active life and were later abandoned, Portencross's concrete structure remains largely intact today. Designed to serve the West Kilbride area, it never established itself as a regular service pier, being restricted to occasional excursion calls – like this one by the CSP's *Duchess of Rothesay*, which put in to Portencross on her way round Arran on Tuesdays and round Ailsa Craig on Fridays. Later in the century, long after the decline of the Clyde steamer fleet, it hosted special calls by *Keppel* in 1983, *The Second Snark* in 1989 and *Waverley* in 1995.

Queen Alexandra pulls away from Fairlie Pier en route to Campbeltown *circa* 1908. In 1901 John Williamson brought out the world's first passenger-carrying turbine steamer, *King Edward*, which was fast enough to run from the upper Firth to the Kintyre port and back in daylight hours. Fairlie gave Williamson a useful train connection on the way down-firth at 10.20am. *King Edward* was so successful that he ordered a bigger, even faster vessel, for the following summer. This was *Queen Alexandra*. The two ships shared Williamson's Campbeltown and Inveraray services until September 1911, when *Queen Alexandra* suffered fire damage. The Canadian Pacific Railway was looking for a fast steamer for its services to Victoria Island and snapped her up, renaming her *Princess Patricia*. A Scottish crew helped to sail her all the way to Vancouver via the South Atlantic and the west coast of the Americas, the 15,000-mile voyage lasting 60 days. Her career on the Pacific lasted another 25 years. Meanwhile, Williamson pocketed the insurance money and built a new, near-identical *Queen Alexandra* in time for the 1912 season.

The pleasures of a seaside holiday are very much to the fore in this tinted postcard dating from shortly before the First World War, when the Clyde steamer fleet was at its apogee and coastal resorts had never had it so good. The steamer is *Atalanta*, the Sou'West's only turbine. Built in 1906 at John Brown & Co's Clydebank yard, she was smaller and slower than the other Clyde turbines and never enjoyed their success, partly because of her tendency to roll. *Atalanta* served as a general purpose vessel, providing back-up on up-firth runs and on the Arran service. On the occasion pictured here, she may have been substituting on the Millport run.

Despite sporadic efforts to attract excursion traffic, the busy cargo port of Irvine never caught on as a calling-place for Clyde steamers. In 1916 some steamers were converted for war service there by the Ayrshire Dockyard and overhaul work continued after the war, with steamers from the railway fleets, MacBraynes and Williamson-Buchanan visiting from time to time. Then, for five winters from 1924, Irvine became the resting place for many of the white-funnelled steamers of Williamson-Buchanan and Turbine Steamers, though the first to arrive – in September 1924 – was actually the paddler *Lord of the Isles*, with distinctive funnels of red, white and black. She lies on the inside of *Eagle III* and astern of the 1912 *Queen Alexandra* (front inside berth) and *King Edward*. In September 1927 the turbine steamer *King George V* suffered a grievous boiler accident as she approached the harbour for lay-up. Though occasional visits for overhaul continued, the end of hibernation at Irvine came in May 1928 when *King Edward* and *King George V* left for their summer duties.

Regular landing excursions by steamer to Ailsa Craig began in 1906, when a Girvan businessman took delivery of *Ailsa*, a 60-ton vessel built at Troon. With her neat lines, yellow funnel and black hull, *Ailsa* was a pretty vessel akin to a steam yacht, capable of berthing at the rock's lighthouse jetty – a possibility denied to larger excursion steamers. Sold to the Cromarty Firth in 1924, *Ailsa* was succeeded by a larger, sturdier looking vessel (*Ailsa II* in her first season, thereafter named *Lady Ailsa*) which undertook the same duties until her sale to France in 1932. Thereafter trips to Ailsa Craig were undertaken by two smaller wooden boats, *Carrick Lass* and the second *Lady Ailsa*.

Juno at Troon in 1923. The stone breakwater dates from 1839-40, when the railway from Glasgow reached the town, but for the following half-century Troon featured little in the Clyde's steamer timetables, other than as a calling point for vessels on their way from Glasgow to the ports of Ayrshire and Wigtownshire. That changed in 1893, when the Sou'West inaugurated a summer excursion programme from Ayr, Troon and Ardrossan, using its new steamer *Glen Rosa*. This ship was succeeded in 1896 by *Neptune*, which was in turn replaced in 1898 by the magnificent *Juno*, which served as Ayr excursion steamer for the remainder of her long career – with the exception of the war years and 1919. *Juno*'s powerful design suited the open sea, while her speed – 19.26 knots on trials on 5 July 1898 – enabled her to sail to the furthest limits of the Firth in the course of a day's work. Her livery in 1923 – the funnel now painted yellow with black top and red band – shows the first signs of that year's amalgamation of the CSP and Sou'West fleets under the London Midland and Scottish Railway (LMS) banner. The following year the Sou'West steamers' lavender grey hulls became black.

"JUNO" AND "GLEN SANNOX" IN AYR HARBOUR

Juno, now in LMS colours, lies ahead of the turbine *Glen Sannox* at Ayr Harbour. The 'Sannox' replaced the paddler of the same name on the Ardrossan-Arran service in 1925. This photograph may date from early August 1930, when she is known to have deputised briefly on the Ayr excursion programme. *Juno* was withdrawn after the 1931 season. The building behind her paddle-box bears the name of the Ailsa Shipbuilding Company Ltd, which built and repaired ships there from 1902 to 1929 on a site previously owned by Samuel McKnight & Co Ltd, the 19th century Ayr shipbuilder. In the late 1940s, under the ownership of the London Graving Dock Company, the yard played host to several Clyde steamers for winter overhaul.

It was uncommon to find two railway steamers berthed together on the outside of Largs Pier. *Glen Rosa* lies next to the pier, with *Duchess of Argyll* coming alongside. It is a morning shot: the rowing boats, hauled up each evening above the reach of high water, will soon be available for hire on the shoreline. In the inter-war period (before her withdrawal in 1938) *Glen Rosa* was often to be found on the Millport run. *Duchess of Argyll*, the Caledonian Steam Packet Company's first turbine, made her debut in 1906 on the Ardrossan-Arran service, but by the late 1920s was more closely associated with the Arran via the Kyles excursion from upper Firth resorts. She remained in service until 1951, after which, stripped of her funnels, she was used by the Admiralty for experimental purposes at Portland, near Weymouth, until 1969.

Given Largs's exposure to north-west winds, steamer captains have always had the option of berthing stern-to-wind on the south corner of the pier, rather than have their ship bumping against the stone face, which did not have the 'give' of a wooden pier. It was a delicate operation, requiring expert ship handling skills – especially, as here, at low tide. The steamer is *Duchess of Fife*, a beautifully proportioned paddler that exemplified pre-1914 Clyde steamer design. The photograph probably dates from the late 1930s, by which time the 'Fife' was being used increasingly on the Millport run – a service she was to become most closely identified with after 1945.

Dalriada was built in 1926 for service between Campbeltown and Glasgow, but Ayr featured occasionally in her schedule. In 1932, for example, she made three calls – on Wednesday 27 April for Ayr Agricultural Show, on Wednesday 15 June to pick up a special party of visitors to the new Auchincruive Agricultural College, and again in July on a Glasgow Fair Monday excursion from Campbeltown. A product of the Port Glasgow yard of Robert Duncan & Co, *Dalriada* was the last steamer built for the Campbeltown and Glasgow Steam Packet Joint Stock Company Limited. Together with *Davaar*, she maintained a year-round connection between the Kintyre port and Glasgow, carrying livestock and cargo as well as passengers. She lacked the yacht-like beauty of her predecessors on the Campbeltown service, but her huge funnel gave her an imposing profile – and with a speed of 17 knots, she was reputedly the fastest single-screw steamer in the world. Her name, chosen by Campbeltown schoolchildren, recalled the ancient kingdom of which Kintyre was a part.

Regular steamer cruising from Girvan did not begin until the early 1890s, when the Glasgow and South Western Railway based one of its fleet at Ayr each summer: this steamer often called at Girvan before proceeding round Ailsa Craig, and some long-distance trips to upper-firth piers were timetabled to begin at Girvan. In the 1930s the town became a destination in its own right – thanks to Williamson-Buchanan Steamers Ltd, which included it in its roster of cruises from Greenock, Dunoon, Rothesay, Largs, Cumbrae and east Arran piers. Among the ships which gave these sailings were the turbines *King Edward* and *Queen Mary*, and the paddler *Queen-Empress*, pictured on one of her Girvan calls in 1932.

Of all the Clyde's steamers, the one based at Ayr invariably had the widest variety of destinations, visiting every corner of the Firth in the course of a three-month season. Such was the popularity of these cruises that the London Midland and Scottish Railway ordered a new turbine for the route in 1932 – and *Duchess of Hamilton*, pictured at Ardrossan Harbour shortly before the Second World War, proved an instant success. In her first season alone, starting with an Invitation Cruise from Ayr on Tuesday 26 June 1932, she undertook trips to Inveraray, Lochgoilhead, Arrochar, Ardrishaig, Campbeltown, Stranraer, Ormidale and Ailsa Craig, plus three sailings from Girvan. On Thursday 31 August 1939, with war looming, *Duchess of Hamilton* gave her last sailing as Ayr excursion steamer. Two days later she undertook the evacuation of children from Ardrossan to Arran and Carradale. After the Second World War she became one of two long-distance excursion steamers based at Gourock.

From the late 19th century until the 1970s, hordes of Scottish holidaymakers passed through Ardrossan every summer en route to the Isle of Man. One of the Isle of Man Steam Packet Company's steamers that transported them in the late 1930s was *Fenella*, here heading gently for a berth in the inner harbour, while the LMS turbine *Marchioness of Graham* embarks passengers for Arran at Winton Pier. *Fenella* and her identical sister *Tynwald*, the first Isle of Man steamers with cruiser sterns, entered service in 1937. Neither survived the Second World War. *Fenella* was sunk by air attack during the evacuation of Dunkirk in May 1940, *Tynwald* by a torpedo off the Algerian coast in November 1942. While Isle of Man steamers were regular summer visitors to Ardrossan, they were not based there – unlike the sleek and beautiful *Lairds Isle* (facing page), which operated the daylight service to Belfast in peacetime from 1933 until her withdrawal in 1957. Built by Denny of Dumbarton in 1911 as *Riviera* for the Southern Railway's cross-channel services to France, she was bought by Burns and Laird in 1933, converted to oil burning and given a new name. Ardrossan folk knew her as 'Smokey Joe', thanks to her habit of emitting black smoke on her departure every morning.

Duchess of Fife lists to port while berthing at Largs at five minutes past five on the afternoon of 26 August 1951. Most of her passengers have gathered on one side in readiness to disembark, and a 'wee ferry' – either *Ashton* or *Leven* – is heading round her stern for the inside of the pier. Much-loved as the Millport steamer in the late 1940s and early 1950s, the 'Fife' is on her way home after the traditional Sunday excursion to Tighnabruaich. Now nearly 50 years old, she will spend one more summer on the run, before being withdrawn and broken up in 1953.

The first post-war sailing from Ayr, on Monday 17 June 1947, was given by *Marchioness of Graham*, which continued as Ayr excursion steamer for the following six summers. Daily cruises to destinations as diverse as Arrochar, Campbeltown, Lochranza, Lochgoilhead and Tarbert were given from Sunday to Thursday, usually involving intermediate piers. In 1954 *Marchioness of Graham* moved to the Ardrossan-Arran run, serving there until the introduction of the car ferry *Glen Sannox* in 1957. That summer she inaugurated the Up River Cruise from Largs to Glasgow, offering holidaymakers at coastal resorts the chance to view the Clyde shipyards, which were still busy with orders from around the world. In 1958 the 'Graham' was sold to Greece, leaving the Clyde with her accommodation stacked with coal for the long voyage to the Mediterranean.

Caledonia, a paddler built by Denny of Dumbarton in 1934, called regularly at Troon from 1954 until the Ayr excursion programme was axed at the end of the 1964 season, and she spent the entire 1954-55 winter there for reboilering and conversion to oil firing. She is pictured on 21 July 1954 – with the funnel of the car ferry *Bute* lying between two harbourside cranes. Construction of the new vessel by the Ailsa Shipbuilding and Engineering Company was well under way at the time: she was launched (facing page) into Troon Harbour on 28 September and entered service on the Wemyss Bay-Rothesay run less than three months later. As the Clyde's first car ferries, *Bute* and her sisters *Arran* and *Cowal* were revolutionary in their day. Previously, cars had to be driven on and off an open deck over precarious wooden planks. The new ferries' design innovations were the garage space forward on the main deck, capable of storing 16 cars, and the side-loading lift amidships, making the routine shipment of vehicles possible at existing piers. The lift was brought up or down to whatever level the tide required, a ramp was lowered and vehicles were driven on or off the vessel. There was no need for a special slipway, and car-carrying sailings could be integrated into the passenger timetable.

In some Clyde resorts, the alternative to a steamer cruise was a shorter trip in one of the beautifully maintained wooden launches that operated from jetties on the beach near the pier. Such was the case at Largs in the 1950s and 1960s. In this morning portrait, the moored launches steal the limelight from *Marchioness of Lorne*, which has just called on her way from Millport to Wemyss Bay. Built by Fairfields in 1935 for the Holy Loch run from Gourock, the 'Lorne' was one of five LMS steamers with concealed paddle-boxes, a curious 1930s design innovation apparently intended to create the impression that they were propeller-driven ships. No one was fooled. *Marchioness of Lorne* was smaller than the others – and slower. That did not matter on the Holy Loch run, but when she became Millport steamer in 1953 in succession to the much-loved *Duchess of Fife*, Cumbrae folk voiced their displeasure loudly. Laid up at the end of the season, the neat little 'Lorne' was sent to the breakers at Port Glasgow after less than 20 years' service.

Carrick, a steam bucket dredger, was a permanent feature of the Ayr Harbour scene from 1938 until the late 1960s. Her job was to clear silt from the mouth of the River Ayr, using a rotating chain of buckets which excavated the underwater sediment and deposited it on board until the ship could discharge its load at sea. One of many specialist craft built by William Simons & Co of Renfrew, *Carrick* was commissioned by the London Midland and Scottish Railway, and later owned by the Docks and Inland Water Executive. She was sold to Palermo, Sicily, in 1968 and registered there as *S Caterina* until broken up in 1984.

Jeanie Deans (this page) and *Talisman* (facing page) were both built in the 1930s by the London and North Eastern Railway for its services out of Craigendoran on the north bank of the Clyde. Apart from occasional visits by 'Jeanie' to Largs and Ayr in the 1930s, when she was the LNER's long-distance cruise steamer, Ayrshire ports did not feature much in their itineraries until later in their careers, by which time they had exchanged their original red, white and black funnel colouring for the standard yellow with black top of the nationalised British Railways. Both these photographs at Largs date from the early 1960s, when *Talisman* was the established Millport steamer and 'Jeanie' was working week-about with *Waverley* on the cruise roster from Craigendoran. This brought her to Largs for the Monday Arran via the Kyles excursion, the Wednesday cruise Round the Lochs and Firth of Clyde and the Friday Up River Cruise, the last-named giving holidaymakers at Clyde resorts an opportunity to see the teeming shipyards of Clydebank and Govan and do some shopping in Glasgow, before returning by train or steamer in the late afternoon. This period was the 'last hurrah' of the Clyde steamers, when economic pressures were forcing a rationalisation of the fleet. 'Jeanie' was withdrawn in September 1964 and, after two unsuccessful summers on the Thames, was broken up in Belgium in 1967. *Talisman* lasted until the autumn of 1966 and ended up at the breakers in Dalmuir the following year.

Ashton and *Leven* were the 'wee ferries' giving a shuttle service in summer between Millport and Largs from 1946 until 1964. They invariably spent the night alongside each other at the Cumbrae pier, but it was unusual to see them together like this at Largs – on 6 June 1964, during their last summer on the run. Built by Denny of Dumbarton for the Caledonian Steam Packet Company in 1938, they were designed to give short cruises on the River Clyde during the Empire Exhibition. After the Second World War they proved useful passenger carriers and lively sea boats on the Cumbrae service. Boarding was by a landing platform and steep staircase, and you paid your fare to a member of the crew who went round the deck with a portable ticket machine. Instead of a funnel, the 'wee ferries' had exhausts at the stern, the fumes from which did not deter passengers from sitting on the little quarter-deck aft. They were succeeded at Millport in 1965 and 1966 by *Countess of Breadalbane* (facing page), another diesel-engined Denny product, which began life as a white-hulled excursion 'steamer' on Loch Awe in 1936 before being brought over to the Clyde by road in 1952. This photograph of her perched against the inside knuckle of Largs Pier dates from the late 1950s, when she was used for a variety of short cruises around the upper Firth. After her 1965-66 Millport service she became the Holy Loch vessel. Sold in 1971 to Gourock ferrymaster Roy Ritchie, she ended her days on Loch Lomond as *Countess Fiona*, and was broken up at Balloch in 1999.

Duchess of Montrose at Ayr on 26 June 1964, with the Isle of Man Steam Packet Company's *Manxman* further upstream. *Duchess of Montrose* and her younger sister *Duchess of Hamilton* were household names to generations of holidaymakers who spent part of their summer on the Clyde coast from the 1930s to the 1960s. The 'Montrose' introduced one-class travel to the Clyde fleet in 1930, and was the Caledonian Steam Packet Company's flagship until the war, cruising to all corners of the Firth, including Ayr and Stranraer. After the war she seemed a shadow of her former self, and various explanations for this have been offered – bad coal, poor wartime maintenance and a succession of masters who did not show her at her best. In 1963 and 1964, however, she perked up under Captain John Macleod (inset), who restored her to her former glory. In the 1950s and 60s the Friday excursion to Ayr was usually undertaken by the 'Hamilton', so this was an isolated visit by *Duchess of Montrose* in her final season.

After spending her eight pre-war summers as Ayr excursion steamer, *Duchess of Hamilton* joined *Duchess of Montrose* at Gourock in 1946, sharing the long-distance cruise roster. Thanks largely to Captain Fergus Murdoch, her master from 1946 to 1967, the 'Hamilton' came across as the faster and more efficient vessel, for which the 'Montrose' was no match – until 1963 and 1964. In those two summers Captain John Macleod 'made the ship go', especially on Friday mornings when the two turbines engaged in their legendary races between Rothesay and Largs. Departure time from Rothesay was the same for both ships, 10.15, with the 'Hamilton' bound for Brodick and Ayr, the 'Montrose' for Lochranza and Campbeltown – but the 'Hamilton' always had the advantage because she was scheduled to leave Largs five minutes earlier than the 'Montrose'. On some occasions, smoke belching from her funnels, the 'Montrose' threatened to overhaul her rival, before hanging back on the approach to Largs. This photograph of the 'Hamilton' at Largs is taken from the 'Montrose' after their very last race on 28 August 1964. Three days later the 'Montrose' was laid up and the following year she was towed to Belgium for breaking up.

Judging by this photograph, taken on Sunday 23 August 1970, you could imagine Fairlie was in the midst of an Indian summer, with three steamers lining up at the pier. Wrong: little more than a year later, the pier was closed for good. This was *Duchess of Hamilton*'s final season. She is pictured here on her return voyage from Campbeltown, and the transfer of her Cumbrae passengers to *Keppel* was under way. As soon as the 'Hamilton' departed for Largs, Rothesay, Dunoon and Gourock, *Maid of Ashton* took her place – having just arrived from Millport after performing the traditional Sunday afternoon excursion to the Kyles of Bute.

The summer of 1970 saw two novelties on the Clyde scene – the debut of a 60-seater 'sidewall' hovercraft, *HM2-011*, and the inauguration of a car ferry service linking Fairlie, Brodick and Tarbert, with additional calls at Millport and Largs. The cars occupying the length of Largs Pier are about to board *Cowal* on her evening run to Millport: it would be another two years before the short shuttle service to Cumbrae Slip would open. *HM2-011*, also operated by the Caledonian Steam Packet Company, was a quieter version of the privately owned hovercraft that had created so much noise at Largs and other coastal towns in 1965. *HM2-011* was no more successful, running at a loss in 1970-71 before being sold.

For tens of thousands of holidaymakers in the 1960s, the journey to paradise – Arran – began on *Glen Sannox*. Berthing overnight at Fairlie, she did mid-morning and mid-afternoon runs from Ardrossan, but returned to Fairlie at midday and in the evening. Car owners waited patiently in line before being beckoned forward onto the side-loading ship, where a hydraulically operated lift with turntables took a handful of vehicles down to the main deck, there to be garaged. The process was slow by modern standards, and *Glen Sannox*'s lift often caused problems, but it was infinitely safer and less nerve-wracking than the old system of driving onto a pair of bare wooden planks running from the end of the pier to the deck below. *Glen Sannox* revolutionised vehicle traffic to Arran when she came out in 1957, but in 1970 she was replaced by a drive-through ferry and transferred to the shorter Gourock-Dunoon and Wemyss Bay-Rothesay routes, to which she was less suited. From 1979 to 1983 she served as CalMac's cruise vessel, but right up to her withdrawal in 1989 she often deputised on the Arran run, always receiving a warm 'welcome home'.

Along with the Arran ferry, the vessel most frequently seen at Ardrossan from the late 1960s to the mid 1970s was Burns and Laird's *Lion*, pictured (left) at Belfast's Donegall Quay in 1968 next to Belfast Steamship Co's *Ulster Queen* (centre) and Coast Lines' *Scottish Coast* (right). Built in 1967-68 and beautifully designed, *Lion* was the first purpose-built car ferry to sail between Ayrshire and Northern Ireland – a response on one hand to declining traffic on Burns and Laird's overnight passenger-and-cargo services from Glasgow, and on the other to the growing success of the shorter Stranraer-Larne route. Operating from Ardrossan's 'Irish berth', *Lion* offered a drive-through daylight service but failed to win the hoped-for traffic. The withdrawal of the service in 1976 signalled the end of Ardrossan's regular sea link with Northern Ireland.

Facing page: unlike *Duchess of Montrose*, *Duchess of Hamilton* was built with a bow rudder – a useful accessory for a steamer built for cruising out of Ayr, where the harbour has a long narrow entrance, sometimes with a strong river flow. In the post-war era, when the 'Hamilton' was based at Gourock, she became closely associated with the Friday excursion to Brodick and Ayr, from where she would give an afternoon cruise round Holy Isle before retracing her path back up-firth. This photograph dates from her penultimate visit to Ayr, on 14 August 1970, and shows deckhands Dougie McGilp and Eddie Mathieson at the bow wheel, taking orders from the bridge as the steamer went astern out of the harbour. The 'Hamilton' made her final call there on 21 August and was withdrawn from service the following month. After a failed attempt to convert her into a floating restaurant, she was broken up at Troon in 1974.

Above: on Saturday 29 April 1967 *Duchess of Hamilton* made the first visit to Girvan by a Clyde steamer since before the Second World War. As Ayr excursion steamer in the 1930s, the 'Hamilton' had made her first visit to Girvan in 1932, her inaugural season, leaving at 8.15am for Ayr, Ardrossan, Keppel, Largs and Round the Lochs, with time ashore at Dunoon. The following year she broke new ground with a cruise to Ardrishaig, but her most ambitious venture was a sailing from Girvan to Inveraray on Games Day, Wednesday 16 August 1933, repeated in 1937. Her final pre-war call was on Saturday 16 August 1939, leaving at 4.30pm on her homeward run to Ayr. The Caledonian Steam Packet Company's post-war managers evidently had no faith in the town's 'pulling power' for excursionists. The occasion for the 1967 visit was a Clyde River Steamer Club charter from Gourock, Largs and Ayr. It was to be another 11 years before Girvan received its next steamer call – by *Waverley* in June 1975, in her first year of operational preservation.

The Isle of Man Steam Packet Company's flagship *Lady of Mann* bids farewell to Ardrossan on Sunday 15 August 1971, on her last public sailing. She reached Douglas, her home port, six hours later, and after a final day there, departed for lay-up at Barrow-in-Furness, where she had been built in 1931. On 31 December 1971 she arrived back on the Clyde under tow for breaking up at Arnott Young & Co, Dalmuir, looking a shadow of her former self. But when she manoeuvred out of Ardrossan's inner harbour on that glorious August morning, and glided 'full astern' towards the open sea, who would have thought this was a final farewell? *Lady of Mann* made a magnificent, unforgettable sight as she turned and sped off in the direction of Ailsa Craig. Built for her owners' services to Liverpool and Fleetwood, she gave outstanding service to her country during the Second World War, especially at the 1940 Dunkirk evacuation, where she lifted more troops to safety than any other vessel. Unlike most of her fleetmates, *Lady of Mann* was an infrequent visitor to Ayrshire, and her many English fans were miffed that her final sailing had not been reserved for them.

Clansman at Ardrossan in 1977. In January 1973 the Clyde fleet of the Caledonian Steam Packet Company was merged with the West Highland fleet of David MacBrayne Ltd to form Caledonian MacBrayne. The outward sign of this was the standardisation of funnel colours: all ships now had red funnels with lions on a yellow disc. Hebridean ferries started appearing on the Clyde and vice versa, and the pace of modernisation was accelerated to take account of booming car ownership and vehicle traffic. Some side-loading ferries were modified for end-loading, and the MacBrayne ferry *Clansman*, not yet 10 years old, was reconstructed at Troon for drive-through operation, emerging in 1973 with an elongated bow that spoiled her appearance. In 1976 she became the summer Arran ferry, for which her enlarged capacity proved useful. But she was underpowered for her new, unwieldy shape and in windy conditions she made heavy weather of the entrance to Ardrossan Harbour. After a series of mechanical problems she was withdrawn in 1984.

By 1975, when this photograph was taken, the Largs-Cumbrae Slip crossing had become the main route to Millport, and the vessel that had inaugurated the run just three years earlier – the former Skye ferry *Coruisk* (foreground) – was needing regular back-up from members of the so-called 'Island' class of bow-loading ferries, which were built in the early and mid 1970s for CalMac's short crossings up and down the west coast. Two of them, *Kilbrannan* and *Morvern*, feature in this busy scene. The vessel on the outside berth is *Glen Sannox*. A stranger to Largs in her early career, the former Arran ferry was seen more frequently there from the mid 1970s. Then, after being re-engined and modernised in 1976-77, she became CalMac's cruise 'steamer', regularly visiting the Kyles of Bute, Arran and Campbeltown. For this purpose her car deck was transformed into a 'sun deck' with umbrellas, deck chairs and a caravan-like bar – not quite the success that was intended, due to windy conditions and seagull droppings.

Three of CalMac's new ships in the 1970s were built at Troon by the Ailsa Shipbuilding & Engineering Company Ltd – *Isle of Cumbrae* (1976) for the Largs-Cumbrae Slip run, *Lochmor* (1979) for the Small Isles service from Mallaig and *Saturn*, pictured immediately after her launch on 30 June 1977. *Saturn* was designed for the Wemyss Bay-Rothesay service but did not take up the run until February 1978, having lain in Troon Harbour for three months after launch while defects in her propeller shafts were sorted. She was the third and last of the Clyde 'streakers' (ferries renowned for their speed, sleek profile and manoeuvrability), and the only one with open passenger deck space forward of the bridge. After spending most of her career on up-firth ferry runs, *Saturn* became a regular visitor to Ardrossan from 2005 until her withdrawal in 2011, providing a supplementary service to Brodick during peak traffic periods in the summer.

Waverley made only two visits to Irvine – on 22 August 1978 and on 18 August 1980, both for the Marymass Festival there. Sold by CalMac for £1 to the Paddle Steamer Preservation Society in 1974, *Waverley* returned to service in 1975 with a more varied programme of excursions than she had given under state control, and Ayrshire ports featured prominently. On that first visit to Irvine in 1978, she took 750 passengers on a non-landing cruise to Holy Isle, and needed a tug to assist her departure stern-first. On her 1980 visit she gave a cruise to Brodick, and left Irvine Harbour bow-first. The creation of the 'Inventors Bridge' across the harbour entrance in the late 1990s, intended to service the now defunct 'Big Idea' building on the Ardeer Peninsula, ended hopes of any more steamer visits.

The 1970s 'Island' class of CalMac ferries ventured where bigger vessels could not go – including Ailsa Craig, which *Rhum* first visited on Tuesday 13 September 1988. The previous evening at Largs she had loaded a caravan, a bulldozer, a forklift tractor and pallets, which she landed on the island's shingle beach. She spent the next few days ferrying more equipment from Girvan, before heading back to Largs on Saturday 17 September. In late August the following year *Rhum* made a return visit to Ailsa Craig, transporting Caterpillar diggers, oil barrels and accessories from Largs and taking granite boulders back to Girvan. She even stayed the night at the exposed rock on Tuesday 29 August. This photograph shows her there on 15 September 1988.

On Saturday 9 May 1987 *Glen Sannox* undertook a 30th birthday cruise from Gourock to Troon and Stranraer – one of several unusual excursions organised in the 1980s and 90s by CalMac's Marketing Officer, Walter Bowie. Although *Glen Sannox* had been built at Troon and frequently received her annual overhaul there, she had never made a commercial visit, and her trip to Stranraer was also a 'first'. Described as 'a tenement on a bathtub' when she made her debut on the Arran run in 1957, *Glen Sannox* ended up as one of CalMac's most popular and versatile vessels, renowned for her speed and spaciousness. She was sold to the Red Sea in 1989.

Facing page: Largs Pier was rebuilt in 2008-09 to create a wider entrance and more secure overnight berthing for the Cumbrae ferry. The £6m project involved demolishing the Victorian stone quay, dredging the surrounding area and creating a new concrete structure 15 metres further into the water. It was carried out with minimal interruption to ferry services, though *Waverley* had to use Fairlie Quay for the early part of her 2009 season. HRH The Princess Royal opened the new pier on Thursday 10 September 2009.

Thanks to *Waverley*, the tradition of steamer cruises from Girvan to Ailsa Craig continues, but she is not the only pleasure steamer to have visited the south Ayrshire port in the 21st century. *Balmoral* has also done so. Built at Cowes in 1949 for the Southampton-Isle of Wight service and purchased by *Waverley*'s owners in 1989 as a back-up for the paddler, she last called on 31 August 2012 en route to Campbeltown, Colonsay and Oban.

Owned since 2014 by a Bristol-based charity, *Balmoral* returned to the Clyde in 2016 and 2017 for a short programme of excursions but struggled to cover her costs. Her 2017 visit at the Glasgow September weekend included a trip to Lochranza and Campbeltown, and while picking up passengers at Largs, she found herself surrounded by three CalMac ferries – *Loch Riddon*, *Loch Linnhe* and *Loch Shira*. The first two have operated the Cumbrae Slip crossing at various times since their debut in 1986, and the larger *Loch Shira* became the dedicated vessel on the service in 2007.

In the late 20th and early 21st centuries, the ferries most closely associated with Ardrossan have been *Isle of Arran* (left) and *Caledonian Isles,* pictured there together on 11 July 2014. Built in 1984 and 1993 respectively, each has marked an advance in capacity on the Arran service, reflecting the rapid growth in traffic that they and their predecessors have stimulated. Since 2005 one vessel alone has not been considered enough to cope with the volume of vehicles in summer, and in 2012 *Isle of Arran* returned as back-up on the crossing for which she was built. Unlike *Caledonian Isles* she has served on most other routes in the CalMac network. In January 2018 she provided a reminder of the 'good old days' of Clyde cruising by undertaking a special Round Arran charter from Ardrossan for the Clyde River Steamer Club.